LAWYER'S GUIDE TO CHEATING, STEALING, AND AMASSING OBSCENE WEALTH

Your failure to buy this book shall not constitute a waiver on the part of the author and/or publisher and/or bookseller (and/or anybody else who wants to get in on this) to a claim for the full retail value of this treatise, plus whatever exemplary or punitive damages the court may award, or the proportionate part thereof which shall be equal to or greater than the amount of free amusement you obtained while browsing through this book in the bookstore.

Please leave your name and address with the clerk at the cash register so that we can tie you up in protracted litigation for the rest of your life in a court located several thousand miles from your home.

Or else, just buy the book!

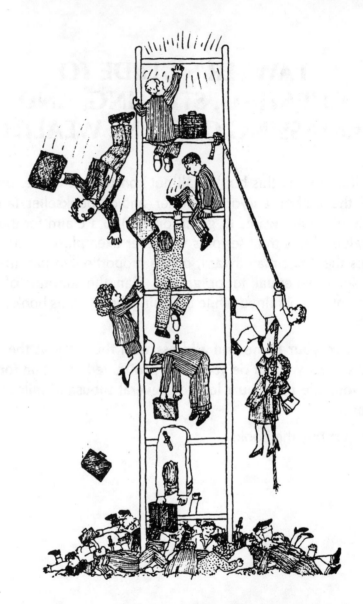

Clawing to the top of the lawyer ladder.

LAWYER'S GUIDE TO CHEATING, STEALING AND AMASSING OBSCENE WEALTH

An Impolite Brief on the Legal Profession

Text
ELLIOTT EGAN, Esq.

Illustrated by
JERRY O'BRIEN

St. Martin's Press
New York

Library of Congress Cataloging-in-Publication Data

Egan, Elliott.
    The lawyer's guide to cheating, stealing, and amassing obscene wealth / Elliott Egan ; illustrated by Jerry O'Brien.
        p.   cm.
    "A Thomas Dunne book."
    ISBN 0-312-07861-7
    1. Lawyers—United States—Humor.   I. Title.
K184.E38   1992
349.73'0207—dc20   92-3085
[347.3000207]   CIP

First published in Ireland by The O'Brien Press Ltd.

First U.S. Edition: July 1992
10 9 8 7 6 5 4 3 2 1

CONTENTS

DISCLAIMER

This book is not intended to depict any actual incident or portray any real attorney-at-law, living or dead. It is not meant to defame or damage the reputation of an ancient and honorable profession. It is meant only for entertainment. Nevertheless, it is recommended that before visiting a lawyer one should remove one's watch and all jewelry, and carefully place wallet or handbag out of harm's way.

In fact, any resemblance between the characters or situations portrayed here and any actual lawyer, living or deceased, is purely coincidental. I made all this stuff up – I swear to God. I never saw anybody actually do any of these things – really!

Elliott Hunt

The Male Lawyer

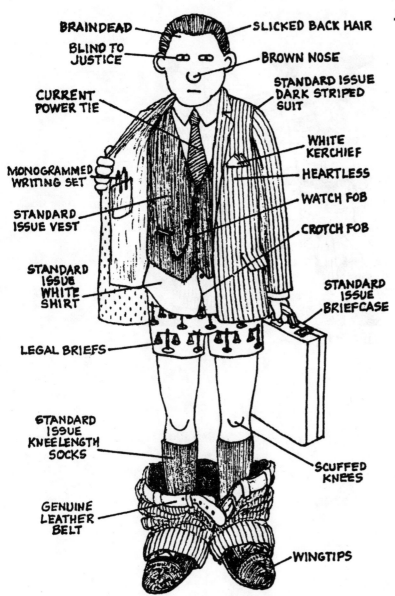

BRAINDEAD

SLICKED BACK HAIR

BLIND TO JUSTICE

BROWN NOSE

STANDARD ISSUE DARK STRIPED SUIT

CURRENT POWER TIE

WHITE KERCHIEF

MONOGRAMMED WRITING SET

HEARTLESS

WATCH FOB

STANDARD ISSUE VEST

CROTCH FOB

STANDARD ISSUE WHITE SHIRT

STANDARD ISSUE BRIEFCASE

LEGAL BRIEFS

STANDARD ISSUE KNEELENGTH SOCKS

SCUFFED KNEES

GENUINE LEATHER BELT

WINGTIPS

The Female Lawyer

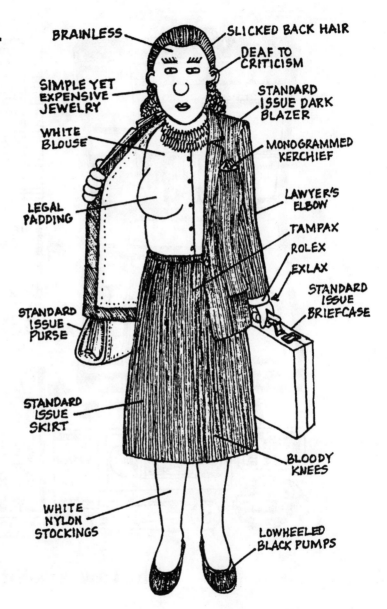

BRAINLESS

SLICKED BACK HAIR

DEAF TO CRITICISM

SIMPLE YET EXPENSIVE JEWELRY

STANDARD ISSUE DARK BLAZER

WHITE BLOUSE

MONOGRAMMED KERCHIEF

LEGAL PADDING

LAWYER'S ELBOW

TAMPAX

ROLEX

EXLAX

STANDARD ISSUE BRIEFCASE

STANDARD ISSUE PURSE

STANDARD ISSUE SKIRT

BLOODY KNEES

WHITE NYLON STOCKINGS

LOWHEELED BLACK PUMPS

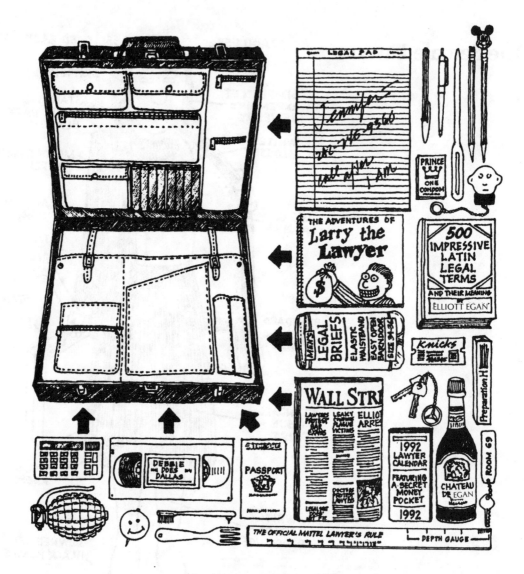

The Lawyer's Kit

CHAPTER 1

Deciding to Become a Lawyer
APTITUDE TEST

Do you have the necessary skills and inclinations to be numbered among the select few who comprise the legal profession?

Take this aptitude test and find out!

Instructions: Following is a set of multiple choice questions. Select the answer A, B or C which would best describe your reaction to the problem posed in the question, or else simply copy the answers which are being filled in by the person to your right. But first make sure that *he* isn't copying *you*!

Question 1

You are awakened in the middle of the night by the shrill sounds of screaming. As you gradually become conscious, you realize that the screams are those of your neighbor lady, Mrs Thatcher, and that her husband is drunk again and giving her one hell of a beating. Thump! Thump! Whack! Whack! In response to the fury of the thrashing, you:

A Call the police and then rush to Mrs T's aid, knowing that Mr Thatcher is twice your size and likely to kill you, but nevertheless being unable to allow that poor woman to endure any more pain.

B Put in your ear plugs and try to get back to sleep. How inconsiderate of Mr Thatcher not to wait until morning!

C Visit Mrs Thatcher in the intensive care unit of the hospital the following day to discuss taking a civil action against both the bar which served Mr Thatcher before he gave the beating, and the sporting goods company which manufactured the baseball bat that Mr Thatcher used to beat her.

Question 2

You go into a news stand to purchase your morning paper on the way to your law office. The man behind the counter is very old and feeble and a bit addled as well. You hand him a five dollar bill to pay for the newspaper. He puts it into the cash register and then is distracted by another customer's question. He turns to give you your change but has obviously forgotten what you gave him. 'Sir,' he inquires, 'was that a five or a ten?'
You:

A Smile patiently at the old gaffer and reply that it was only five dollars and thank him for his many years of service to you and your family.

B Seize the opportunity presented and reply without hesitation 'Ten dollars.'

C Draw yourself up in utter indignation and exasperation and shout: 'You stupid old fool! What are you trying to pull here? It was a twenty!'

Question 3

You are on your way to the racetrack when you discover that seated behind you on the bus are the owner and trainer of Greased Lightning, a horse with a rather unimpressive track record which would be more accurately named something like 'Anchored Three-legged Tortoise'. They are in a heated but whispered discussion, which you can barely hear by leaning all the way back in your seat, about how the contest is fixed and Greased Lightning is a sure bet to win in the fifth race. You:

A Shake your head in disbelief at the dishonesty of these two men who would dare to debase such an ancient and worthy sport, and decide to skip the races that day and instead go to church and offer thanks to God for your own honesty.

B Rush off to the bank and withdraw everything you have and make it to the racetrack just in time for the fifth race where you bet everything on Greased Lightning.

C Call several of your richest clients and tell them that you have heard an unconfirmed report that Sucker's Bet is going to win in the fifth race, and offer them the professional courtesy of covering their bets (large amounts only, of course – at least $50,000) should they not be able to withdraw sufficient funds in time to make it to the track. After you have received commitments for at least a million dollars on Sucker's Bet, you pay a stable boy ten dollars to slip the horse a 'mickey', just to make sure, and then buy yourself a drink and relax while watching the fifth race and planning your retirement on the Riviera.

Question 4

Your closest friend calls you in the middle of the night and says: 'Look, I've got a terrible problem! I just killed a man in a bar fight that spilled into the alleyway. Fortunately, no one saw me do it and I got away clean. But I dropped my wallet in the alley and I need someone to go back there and get it for me, otherwise the police will have it! Can you help me?' You:

A Knowing full well the risk you are taking of becoming an accessory, decide that you can't forsake your friend in his time of need. You rush to the alleyway and retrieve the wallet before the police arrive. But you also insist that your friend arrange for a long course of spiritual counselling so that he will never harm another person again as long as he lives!

B Curse your friend for calling so late and try to get back to sleep.

C You rush to the alleyway so that you can get the money out of your friend's wallet before the police find it and send him to prison for the rest of his life.

Question 5 (men only)

The 18-year-old daughter of your best friend, a perfectly innocent man who was executed for murder several years earlier after you botched his defense in court because you were drinking heavily during the trial, has called you and stated that she will be visiting prospective colleges in your area and has asked if she could stay with you and your family. Your charming and overweight wife and seven bratty children, as it turns out, are vacationing several thousand miles away and fortunately cannot be reached. You recall that your late friend's daughter is an exceptionally rare beauty and has served as both homecoming queen and captain of the cheerleaders in her local high school. You fondly recall the Christmas card photos of her in her short tight cheerleader's outfit as she shook her little pompoms for the camera. Not wanting to seem inhospitable, you invite her to stay with you. As the taxi brings her from the airport, you shower, apply cologne and don your leather smoking jacket which was last in style in 1957.

After she arrives, you decant that very old and very expensive bottle of burgundy which you and your wife have been saving for a special occasion (what could be more special than this?) and pan grill a couple of tenderloin steaks and some mushrooms. After a cozy dinner by the fire, she looks across the table at you with those liquid brown eyes of hers which so beautifully complement her long and golden hair and says, 'Uncle Jimmy, you're always here when I need you, and now that I'm a woman, can I do anything to repay you?'

After your heartbeat drops back down to less than 200 beats per minute, you:

A Explain to her that at such a young age it's very easy to get one's feelings all confused and that you love her just like a daughter and that those feelings are what make yours such a special relationship.

B   Struggling against the almost unbearable temptation which has been placed before you in the form of this steamy, sensuous and wine-besotted young lady, you finally succumb to her wiles and as you carry her in your arms to the bedroom, you look towards the heavens and cry, 'God help me, Charlie, and you were my best friend!'

C   You look her straight in the eye and reply, 'Yes, Kelly, I *will* sleep with you and if it's really good, I'll even forget about the balance which your father owes me from the trial!'

Question 6 (women only)

You and your college roommate, Muffy, have just begun the second semester of your freshman year. The women outnumber the men by three to one on your campus, so getting a boyfriend isn't easy. You are both wild about Jimmy, a tall, dark and handsome senior who is captain of the football team. Jimmy is a very rough player who really gets into the thick of things out on the field, and so has suffered several hundred hard blows to the head. He is now unable to distinguish between animate and inanimate objects and can only wear shoes which fasten with velcro. Despite the fact that Jimmy cannot tell either you or Muffy apart from the radiator (he fondles the radiator while he sits on Muffy to warm himself), you are both intent on having him sire your children in order that his defective genetic message will be passed on to the next defenseless generation.

After being shown (for the twenty-third time) how to use the telephone by his fraternity brother Butch, Jimmy calls your room looking for Muffy, or at least the radiator. Knowing that she is gone for the weekend to attend her mother's funeral, you:

A   Tell Jimmy how very happy Muffy will be that he called and tell him how much Muffy cares for him. Then pour yourself a glass of cheap bourbon and have a good cry.

B   Tell Jimmy that *you* are Muffy and that you're feeling very lonely tonight, and a little chilly as well, since you're wearing nothing but a lacy black thong bikini panty and a pair of spike heels.

C   Tell Jimmy that Muffy has gone to a motel to have sex with Butch for the whole weekend and that she told you that she's planning to make up a story about going to her mother's funeral because she says that only Jimmy would be dumb enough to believe it.

Scoring

Give yourself one point for each **A** answer, two points for each **B** answer and three points for each **C** answer.

Results

5-8

There's really no hope for you in the legal profession. You are sentimental and lack objectivity. Try studying philosophy or going into a monastery, or, if you'd like to save us all a lot of trouble, just kill yourself!

9-10

The outlook for a successful career in law for someone like you is quite dim, but not entirely beyond remedial treatment. You have a tendency to try to cling to childish ideals about right and wrong; such concepts are, of course, entirely inappropriate for a lawyer. But you aren't any saint, either, and when push comes to shove, you think of yourself first. Maybe there *is* hope for you after all!

11-12

There is a distinct possibility that you could make a *living* in the law, but not necessarily a *fortune*. On the positive side, you are dishonest and dishonorable, lazy and lascivious, sneaky and sly. Sometimes, however, you'll miss a truly great opportunity just because an easier or more obvious opportunity to make a quick buck presents itself first. Good things come to those who wait. With patience and education, you might just make it.

13-14

Now we're getting into lawyer territory. You are a scoundrel – a true piece of scum! You do things as a matter of course that others wouldn't even fantasize about. You have no principles, no morals and not a single redeeming quality. When you apply to law school, be sure to ask for a full scholarship. Not only do you deserve it, but you'll make your alma mater proud of you in the years to come.

15

There is not a shred of human decency to be found anywhere in you! You would sell your own mother into slavery if you hadn't already evicted her from the family home. You couldn't be trusted within fifty feet of the church poor box at your own wedding. You're the sort of person who would pickpocket a dentist whilst he was cleaning your teeth. You see other people as nothing more than objects to be manipulated for your own ends. How does a Federal judgeship sound to you?

CHAPTER 2

Essential Personality Defects
in the Pre-lawyer Child
PERSONALITY PROFILE

Age 4

Steals coins from grandmother's purse during old lady's naptime. Is caught in the act by mother but denies accusations, claiming that he was only trying to protect coins from a monster seen lurking near closet. Is successful in argument, returns later that afternoon to steal paper money as well.

Age 9

Tells teacher that homework was lost in flash flood on way to school. Teacher expresses doubt, noting clear skies during past three weeks. Pre-lawyer child replies that weather patterns differ significantly in *his* neighborhood. Later that day is caught cheating on test and sent to principal's office. Tells principal that teacher had referred to him as 'a fat slob, a toad of a man', which of course teacher never said. Regardless, teacher is fired and replaced that afternoon. Pre-lawyer child places new teacher on probation and warns her not to mess with him!

Age 13

After learning facts of life begins to sell condoms to classmates for five dollars each, claiming that to even masturbate without one will lead to blindness or death.

Age 19

Caught cheating (again!) on freshman mid-terms, denies accusations and charges proctor with homosexual advances. Sues college but accepts out-of-court settlement for three hundred thousand dollars. Continues with education, and cheats more carefully during remaining three years.

CHAPTER 3

Going into Private Practice

Hiring a Secretary

When hiring a secretary, a young lawyer should remember that there needs to be a certain 'chemistry' between the lawyer and his secretary.

Forget all that stuff about typing and filing and being able to spell 'judge' and knowing that you have to put stamps on letters before you mail them, and all those other technical secretarial details.

After all, since the young lawyer is just starting out he doesn't have any clients anyway, so what difference does it make? The really important thing is that the lawyer and secretary get along well together.

They'll be spending a lot of time together over the next twenty years – working late, working alone, working weekends, going on business trips together, attending social and political events and generally getting to know more about each other than about anyone else.

Occasionally, their relationship may transcend the purely business, and if this happens, they will have to agree on alibis.

BERTHA

- TYPES 250 WORDS PER MINUTE
- MAKES EXCELLENT COFFEE AND TEA
- SPEAKS FIVE LANGUAGES FLUENTLY

PETUNIA

- TYPES 100 WORDS PER MINUTE
- MAKES PRETTY GOOD COFFEE AND TEA
- SPEAKS ENGLISH AND FRENCH

PERCY

- TYPES 50 OR SO WORDS PER MINUTE
- MAKES USUALLY WARM COFFEE AND TEA
- SPEAKS ENGLISH, SORT OF

LISA

- KNOWS WHAT A TYPEWRITER IS
- KNOWS WHAT COFFEE AND TEA ARE
- KNOWS WHEN TO KEEP HER MOUTH SHUT

SecretaryTypes

The following are some of the aptitude tests which may be given to an applicant for a secretary's position. The list is by no means all-inclusive and other tests may be designed by the young lawyer to fit his particular needs.

LAP TEST

Because the young lawyer does not yet have any clients to fleece (see FLEECE in Chapter 7, Legal Dictionary) his office budget will be very modest at the beginning. The provision of a separate chair for his secretary is an extravagance in which no new lawyer should indulge. But she does have to sit somewhere, doesn't she?

As with any new business, the establishment of a law practice demands certain sacrifices from its proprietor. The new lawyer may just have to suffer through the first few years with his secretary's slender and well-muscled legs and perfectly symmetrical buttocks planted firmly on his lap for as many as eight hours each day.

Therefore, it is of utmost importance that the size, texture, fit and body temperature of the secretary be compatible with those of the lawyer. To test this, he must be able to support a potential secretary on his lap for at least one hour.

LYING TEST

To administer the lying test, have the applicant for the secretarial position devise plausible reasons for each of the following situations:

A Why you haven't been home to see your wife or children yet this month.

B Why you failed to appear in court for three consecutive days despite repeated phone calls from the judge's clerk.

C Why you awoke in the gutter yesterday morning with your wallet missing, an awful hangover and the name 'Caroline' tattooed on your forehead.

COFFEE TEST

The young lawyer should realize this: if he works five days a week, forty-eight weeks a year for the twenty years that the secretary works for him, and if he drinks four cups of coffee a day (or tea, if he's an Irish or British lawyer, but in that case he'll be drinking *ten* cups a day, not *four*) that the secretary makes for him, then over the course of her servitude he will consume nineteen thousand, two hundred cups of coffee (or forty-eight thousand cups of tea) that she has made for him. The coffee test, therefore, is terribly important not only for the lawyer himself, but for the clients who will drink the coffee before deciding whether or not to pay the lawyer his retainer. A good cup of coffee has had more to do with the success of most law practices than have all of the degrees and certificates hanging on the lawyer's wall! So don't worry if you didn't go to Harvard – just make sure your coffee is the best and pretty soon guys who went to Harvard will be working for *you*!

Stationery and Business Cards

You may have only one chair and one desk, but that's no reason not to try and make your clients think that you are one of several senior partners in a long-established multi-national firm with the highest credentials and most cherished reputation. All of this can be accomplished with about four hundred dollars worth of stationery and a good imagination! A few friends or relatives in distant cities or even other countries can prove helpful as well.

First, you have to think of a good name for your firm. Four or five stodgy Anglo-Saxon sounding names linked together in random order will usually suffice. Avoid any names that sound too 'foreign' or end in vowels; this will always result in getting less money from clients, or not getting the clients at all.

See opposite page for suggestions on how to name your new law firm.

See how easy it is to name a law firm? This is how they all do it! (You don't really believe all that rubbish about legendary deceased partners from the early 1800s, do you?)

Now that you've named your firm, it's time to choose the major city in which its head offices will be located. London, Berlin, New York and Paris are all acceptable locations; Birmingham (England or Alabama) and Hoboken (New Jersey are not. A prestigious address in New York (for example, Madison Avenue) is worth its weight in gold, and can usually be obtained as a mail drop for a minimal fee.

Next, you locate absolutely the best printer you can possibly find, because your business cards and your stationery are all that most potential clients will ever have to judge you by, and you select the most elegant but intimidating 100% linen stock in an ivory or light gray (never beige or anything that looks warm and thus weak). Have your new firm's name and its very impressive headquarters address boldly engraved at the top, and list yourself as a senior partner at your own branch address.

**If you're too lazy to name your own firm,
just choose one name from each of the columns A, B, C, D
and string them together in any order you choose.**

A	C
Wadsworth	Peterson
Tuttle	Dawson
Yeats	Winthrop
James	Sutherland
Butterfield	Twining
Randolph	Longfellow

B	D
Abercrombie	Churchill
Jackson	Downing
Henry	Adams
Alexander	Knight
Keating	Winston
Smith	Daniels

For example:

(1) Winthrop, Winston, Tuttle & Smith

(2) Butterfield, Adams, Peterson & Knight

(3) Downing, Longfellow, Abercrombie & Randolph

Assembling a Really Impressive Library

The reason why lawyers are able to get so much money from people is that they usually sit the clients down in the law firm's conference room or library when they take the money off them.

This is very intimidating to most people because these rooms have shelves and shelves of ancient and thick and heavy books with rich red burgundy leather bindings and gold-leaf embossed bars across the bindings, and they all have titles like 'Am.Jur.Code Cited Amortized Superior Mumbo-Jumbo Let's Get Rich!' in heavy black lettering.

Now, the first thing that the clients think is that the lawyer has *read* all this stuff and is therefore a great omnipotent force which cannot be denied its fee without invoking the wrath of generations of lawyers past, when the truth is that many lawyers don't even know *how* to read anything other than a check and then they only understand the numbers that follow a dollar sign. And the lawyers that do know how to read haven't got any more of an idea what's inside those books than the clients do. It's true! Just ask yourself: when you go to a dentist to have your teeth drilled, does he leave all his dental school books lying around to show you how smart he is? Of course not!

Anyway, the library is as necessary to the lawyer's art as are silk handkerchiefs and mirrors to the magician's. But a room full of that stuff, especially when you're just starting out and still have to share a chair with your secretary, Miss Thighbury, can be prohibitively expensive. Query: What to do? Fortunately, old lawyers are dying all the time and their greedy widows and children are happy to sell their entire libraries for pennies on the dollar, because the books are all out of date anyway and useless for any purposes other than intimidating your clients. But that's what you want them for, anyhow. So, after paying four hundred dollars for a senior partnership in a venerable old firm, another two hundred dollars will get you the same sort of library (for appearances' sake) that you would have if you really *were* a partner in such a firm!

Now that you've spent your six hundred dollars and hired Miss Thighbury, you're ready to practice law!

Finding New Clients

As a senior partner in a 'long-established multi-national firm', finding new clients shouldn't be any problem at all, as long as you remember this: it is you who is doing the potential client a favor by even so much as talking to him and agreeing to take his money. Never forget this! You will always be meeting people – at social events such as weddings and funerals and baptisms and New Year's Eve parties, at business and political and educational and professional activities, and just by happenstance (such as people you meet who are seated next to you on the bus innocently reading their newspapers when you decide to strike up a conversation about how they got that cast on their leg) – and they will all want legal advice for free. When this happens, look them straight in the eye and say, 'The place for legal counsel is in my library, where all my reference materials are handy and where my secretary, Miss Thighbury, is present to assist me.' Then make an appointment for the client to come to your office, but always study your pocket calendar (which will usually be entirely empty) carefully for a few moments before you say, 'Well, I think I can squeeze you in at 3:45 on the afternoon of ...' and give them an appointment two or even three weeks later. It's amazing how much a truly busy attorney is respected! Pretty soon you'll have potential clients queuing up *fighting* to get into that empty calendar of yours!

Getting Rid of the Garbage

Even though you and Miss Thighbury may be starving, there are *some* clients you just won't want to have under any circumstances. These clients are collectively referred to as 'the garbage'. Individually, they are referred to as 'that guy you threw into the alleyway last week when he forgot to bring his checkbook to the consultation'.

These clients cause trouble from the first time you meet them, and an experienced attorney begins to recognize them even before they speak. They have a certain *odor* to them, a distinctly musty smell like they haven't left the back parlor since the Great War, and they always dress in a peculiar manner, wearing as many as three or four sweaters on a perfectly warm spring day. They will invariably carry with them not one but as many as twenty satchels and brown paper shopping bags filled with a selection of moldy and tattered files and folders and documents and drawings and diagrams and affidavits and half-eaten sandwiches from 1954, and all of this crap together they will refer to as 'my case'.

They will tell you how they have gone to 147 other lawyers to discuss 'my case' and have been turned away by all of them, and then they will ask you if you would mind 'having a look' through 'my case' before quoting a fee, as they certainly have no intention of paying you if after four thousand hours of legal research you find that 'my case' is nothing more than the collected grievances of an octogenarian lunatic.

Now, here is what you will do with such a potential client. You will say: 'Mr Manurebreath, I am sure that you appreciate that a lawyer's time is his stock in trade. You have already taken almost an entire hour of my time this afternoon, for which you will be billed $500 and have a lien placed upon your house if you fail to pay such amount within the next thirty minutes. If you want any additional hours, you must pay me a retainer of $25,000 to compensate me for the time I will spend sorting through this garbage and for the overtime which I will have to pay my groundskeeper to incinerate it when I am through.' At this point, Mr Manurebreath will begin to sputter something about 'all the damned lawyers' and it will be necessary to call Rocco, your chauffeur, to sort things out.

Taking the Retainer off the Client

Have you ever seen a photo of a snake (a very LARGE snake, that is, like a 40-foot python or anaconda) which has just swallowed a horse or water buffalo or something like that? And did you notice how content the snake looked, like he was just drifting off into a 6-month sleep?

That's just the way a lawyer looks after he gets paid his retainer! A retainer (see Chapter 7, Legal Dictionary) is a large sum of money which is paid to a lawyer at the beginning of the client's relationship with the lawyer so that the lawyer will have money to spend while working on the client's behalf. This is necessary because if it were not for the retainers paid to a lawyer, he would not have money to feed and clothe his family, to donate to his church, to pay his bar bills, to keep his mistress, to bribe politicians and judges, and to attend law school at night in order to get a better understanding of how to solve the client's problem and also how to get bigger retainers from other clients in the future.

Taking the retainer off the client is as subtle an art as the seduction of a Victorian virgin. It requires guile, persuasion, luck, seclusion, an appropriate setting, a ready smile, all the right answers, a comfortable place to sit, no

interruptions and, occasionally, a bottle of gin.

Clients are reluctant to give the lawyer his retainer – that's the simple truth of it! They fear that after paying the lawyer five or ten or twenty-five thousand dollars, he's not going to do anything for them. The best way to convince the client otherwise is through simple, logical, calm and cogent reasoning – something like this: 'IF YOU DON'T GIVE ME ALL YOUR MONEY, MR MURPHY, YOU'LL GO TO PRISON FOR THE REST OF YOUR LIFE, YOU'LL LOSE THE FARM, YOUR WIFE WILL HAVE TO SELL HER BODY TO FEED THE CHILDREN, AND ALL YOUR TEETH WILL FALL OUT!' From this quiet and reasoned approach the client will come to fully realize the serious implications of his predicament and be more willing to co-operate with you.

Sometimes, however, a stronger approach will be necessary, and you will need to once again call Rocco, your chauffeur.

CHAPTER 4

Up the Ladder
GETTING TO THE TOP OF THE LAW FIRM

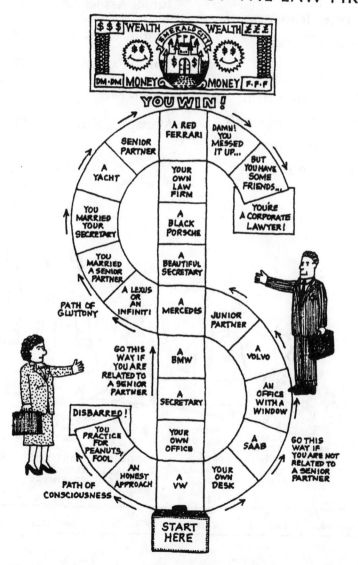

Everything sure looks bright now that you've passed your final exams and been admitted to the bar and gotten a good job offer from one of your city's leading law firms.

So let's take a look at your prospective career with that firm; for the sake of argument (and don't we love to argue?) we'll assume that you are beginning your career at age 25.

Here are the jobs you will hold:

Title	Age at Start	Age at Finish
Junior Associate	25	28
Senior Associate	28	35
Junior Partner	35	45
Senior Partner	45	65
Managing Partner	65	118*

*Approximate age at retirement unless death necessitates an earlier retirement.

However, it is important to note that not all lawyers make their way up the firm's ladder so predictably. The rungs on that ladder are very slippery, and many lawyers fall (or are pushed or kicked) off before they reach the top. It is important to your survival that you learn to do the pushing and kicking yourself. When you begin your career, your pay will be small and your hours will be long. You will lead a wretched existence for many years, the only consolation being the knowledge that somehow, someday, you may be able to inflict such misery on someone else.

Of course, in the event that you are a woman, it is highly unlikely that you will ever be hired in the first place. You must remember that this is entirely reasonable, in the estimation of the managing partners, as you will no doubt, shortly after being hired, marry a ploughman, become pregnant, and leave the boredom of a legal career for the utter thrill and ecstasy of standing by the kitchen sink for the rest of your life and wondering, 'Is today a good day to buy more cabbage?'

But if you are one of those overly aggressive and ambitious females who want more from life than a new set of kitchen utensils every twenty-five years and can convey this greed and selfishness during your interview, you may, in fact, be offered a job. Don't start jumping for joy yet though, as your own career path may be a bit more circuitous than a man's.

Male or female, here's what you can expect.

JUNIOR ASSOCIATE
(gentlemen)

Hours
6:00am - 1:00am, seven days a week.
Total weekly hours – 133.

Salary
$700 per week – approximately $5.26 per hour.

Office
Small, windowless room shared with two other junior associates and furnished with World War II field hospital surplus desks, chairs and shelves in battleship-gray gunmetal with blood stains still evident.

Secretary
Your mother.

On Wall
Flies, chewing gum.

Floor
Gravel.

Beverage
Tepid water from your boy scout canteen.

Plants
Avocado pits in glass jars.

Ventilation
None.

Vermin/Insects
Three mice who eat most of the bugs, fortunately.

JUNIOR ASSOCIATE
(ladies)

Hours
6:00am - 1:00am, seven days a week.
Total weekly hours – 133.

(Not all spent at the office, however. Occasionally, Mr Gooser, the senior partner to whom you report, will ask you to accompany him to the lingerie shop to help him choose a gift which his wife would like. A man's just no good at making those really important decisions alone, you know. Besides, you two are just about the same size. You wouldn't mind trying a few on, would you?)

Salary
$450 per week – approximately $3.38 per hour.

Office
To prevent you from distracting any of the

male associates, you have been assigned to share the broom closet with Grigsby, the ancient handyman.

Secretary

Everybody assumes you *are* the secretary.

On Wall

When Grigsby was young, he put a girlie calendar on the wall. It remains, opened to 'Miss August, 1939'. Grigsby comments often on your similarity in appearance, but notes that Miss August was much better paid.

Floor

You can't figure out what it is, but Grigsby assures you it's been there since the First World War and he's never had a complaint about it.

Beverage

Fortunately, the broom closet has a sink. You make herbal tea with hot tap water each morning. When you're really depressed, Grigsby lets you 'take a chug' from his pocket flask.

Plants

With no window and no ventilation, the potted plants which you bring with you die quickly. Not so with the black and orange fungus which grows abundantly in the cracks and corners!

Ventilation

Grigsby has coughing fits.

Vermin/Insects

None, due to the vast amounts of poison placed strategically around the small room. But you *have* noticed some interesting changes in your own body, including a sudden growth of facial hair.

SENIOR ASSOCIATE

(gentlemen)

Hours

8:00am - 10:00pm, six days a week.
Total weekly hours – 84.

Salary

$1000 per week – approximately $11.90 per hour.

Office

Private interior office furnished with plain wooden desk and bookshelf.

Secretary

Margaret – frumpy and contentious middle-aged woman shared with four other senior associates.

On Wall
The firm's calendar.

Floor
Linoleum.

Beverage
Canned soda.

Plants
Rhododendrons from aunt's garden.

Ventilation
Electric fan.

Vermin/Insects
Private mouse that you don't have to share with anyone.

SENIOR ASSOCIATE
(ladies)

Hours
8:00am - 10:00pm, six days a week.
Total weekly hours – 84.

(Now that you are a senior associate, Mr Gooser no longer requests your presence during his weekly lingerie-buying forays.

Knowing the value of your time and having great respect for your skills and intelligence, he only asks for an occasional neck rub.)

Salary
A modest increase is warranted, young lady! Now you're making $500 a week – approximately $5.95 hourly.

Office
You now have the broom closet to yourself, as Grigsby has been promoted to partner ahead of all the women lawyers, based solely on his possession of a penis. The fact that he has no legal education and can neither read nor write have been deemed irrelevant by the managing partners, who note Grigsby's knowledge of football and grouse hunting in response to your objections.

Secretary
The partners thought it would be nice to assign you a male secretary, and so one day Frank N. Stein appears. He is a huge and slow-moving fellow, with a strangely colored complexion and an apparent indifference to the workings of the law office. The partners were able to get him at a very good price, though, as the state institution where he was previously resident has *paid them* to take him off their hands. You lock him in the coal bin and continue with your own typing.

On Wall
Frank has nailed something to the wall which looks vaguely human, but you're afraid to ask.

Floor
At this point, who cares?

Beverage
Now that he has full use of the partners' club room, Grigsby left his pocket flask behind. You've been filling and draining it with great regularity.

Plants
Gift from Gooser – overgrown venus fly trap. Occasionally, the thing reaches out and nips you on the bottom, but at least it's managed to eat most of the fungus out of the cracks.

Ventilation
A severe storm has blown the roof off; now you have plenty of fresh air and sunshine but often have to work under an umbrella.

Vermin/Insects
With no roof, it's pointless to even list them.

JUNIOR PARTNER
(gentlemen)

Hours
9:00am - 8:00pm, five days a week.
Total weekly hours – 55.

Salary
$1500 per week – approximately $27.27 per hour.

Office
Attractive, well-lit private windowed office with mahogany-veneer desk, bookshelves with glass doors, brass-plated desk lamp.

Secretary
Gwendolyn – fairly attractive and well dressed young woman in mid-twenties, shared with one other junior partner. Dresses conservatively, no hanky-panky but maybe an innocent kiss (no tongue) at the firm's Christmas party.

On Wall
Fox and hounds hunting prints – tasteful but cheap.

Floor
Wood.

Beverage
Gwendolyn makes coffee.

Plants
Miniature palm trees in floor planters.

Ventilation
What are you worrying about ventilation for? You've *got* a window!

Vermin/Insects
Whatever flies or crawls through that window you always wanted.

JUNIOR PARTNER
(ladies)

Hours
9:00am - 8:00pm, five days a week.
Total weekly hours – 55.

(Mr Gooser is now a managing partner, but he's still your boss. But *you're* a partner too, and you don't let Mr Gooser forget it! When he asks you for a neck rub, you politely but firmly reply that such a request is inappropriate in a professional setting. Mr Gooser concedes your point, and promises it won't happen again. Later, he calls a meeting of the managing partners to discuss your insubordination and the upcoming grouse hunting weekend at Grigsby's place in Scotland.)

Salary
Now that you're a junior partner, you're getting paid just what all the other junior partners are getting, Mr Gooser proudly informs you. $700 per week! Close to $12.73 an hour!

Office
They've actually placed you in quite a nice office now, which you share with two other lawyers. Although, you remark when first seeing it, that it seems furnished with World War II field hospital surplus equipment.

Secretary
You don't know who she is, but the old gal is *very nice*. Almost like somebody's *mother*.

On Wall
Now that you're actually in an office with other lawyers, you've decided to put something up on the wall which expresses the real you; it's a poem by an obscure but absolutely wonderful Elizabethan. The guys who share your office read it and then laugh a lot; later, they take it down in order to make space for the football playoff chart.

Floor
It's really very lovely – some sort of mosaic.

Beverage
You no longer need Grigsby's pocket flask. You've been attending A.A. meetings and they've been quite helpful. Now all you need to make you happy is pure, fresh, clean water. Too bad there isn't any!

Plants
You're a partner now, you don't have time to be wasting on plants.

Ventilation
An occasional little breeze when the guys rush out the door and head for the pub.

Vermin/Insects
Those two guys you share the office with.

SENIOR PARTNER
(gentlemen)

Hours
10:00am - 6:00pm, four days a week.
10:00am - 1:00pm, Fridays.
Total weekly hours – 35.

Salary
$3000 per week – approximately $85.71 per hour.

Office
Very impressive double-windowed private chamber with adjoining private reception area. Designed according to your specifications by local architect. Solid mahogany desk, bookshelves and panelling. Solid brass desklamps, marble ashtray, upholstered couch, cocktail table.

Secretary
Debbie – quite a little number and you don't have to share her with anyone! Usually 22, she has just graduated from a well-thought-of local college and is considering her options, among them marriage to a successful, middle-aged lawyer. Is bright, pretty, articulate and extremely affectionate. Wears very short skirts and is always bending *way* over to get something out of the bottom file drawer. Calls you 'Mr So-and-so' in the presence of others, 'Daddy' when the two of you are alone. Likes to sit on your lap, especially on those chilly autumn days. Tries hard to please. Will do *anything* for you.

On Wall
Massive seascape in oil by renowned nineteenth-century painter.

Floor
Chinese carpet over solid cherry floorboards.

Beverage
Full liquor cabinet.

Plants
Japanese bonsai arrangement.

Ventilation
Air conditioning.

Vermin/Insects
None, fortunately.

Senior Partner
(ladies)

You didn't *really* think you'd be made a senior partner after talking that way to Mr Gooser ten years ago, did you?

Managing Partner
(gentlemen only)

Hours
11:00am - 4:00pm, four days a week.
Never on Fridays.
Total weekly hours – 20.

Salary
$12,000 per week – approximately $600 per hour.

Office
Private outer reception area leads to private inner reception area leads to private outer office leads to corridor leads to stairs leads to private inner office suite of six rooms, abounding in burgundy leather couches, heavy deep gold drapes, crystal chandeliers, strange-looking primitive *objets d'art* with oversized phallic representations, a full-wall movie screen, a twelve-foot desk carved from a single piece of bird's-eye maple and inlaid with 24-karat gold, and a sixty-foot waterfall cascading from the ceiling of your private dining room.

Secretary
Danielle – sent to you just this morning (you like them fresh!) by a top Parisian modelling agency, she is 5'11" in her bare feet (you've already taken her measurements so that you may order her various fantasy costumes, including the French maid's uniform and schoolgirl-style plaid skirt), slender, blond, blue-eyed and beautiful. At 19, she's as innocent and wide-eyed as a doe. She doesn't type, thinks that 'filing' means attending to her fingernails, and still hasn't been able to figure

out which end of the telephone to hold to her ear and which end to speak into. But that's all right; you'll teach her all of that and *so much more*. Danielle lives to please you – in fact, she lives with you! By this time you have left your overweight and overbearing wife and obnoxious children and everything else connected with the country estate that you worked all these years to acquire, and are now living in a smaller but comfortable six-bedroom brownstone in the city. In another month, Danielle will be gone, and the modelling agency will supply another fresh young lady to distract you yet again.

On Wall
Reclining nude by seventeenth-century old master, valued at three million dollars.

Floor
Highly-polished Italian marble covered by antique Persian carpet.

Beverage
Champagne sipped from Danielle's high heels.

Plants
Adjoining three-acre English garden.

Ventilation
Danielle's hot breath on your naked body.

Vermin/Insects
Who cares?

CHAPTER 5
Schedule of Fees

What You Pay	What You Get
$500	The lawyer's contempt and a bill for $500 more.
$1000	A hearty handshake.
$1500	A calendar (last year's) advertising the lawyer's services.
$2500	Three of your phone calls returned.
$5000	An authentic letter, typed by the lawyer's secretary on his official letterhead, thanking you for the $5000.
$10,000	Some legal thinking by the lawyer about a small matter or two, but nothing actually resolved.
$25,000	A minor matter (such as a parking ticket or a dispute with your landlord) resolved by the lawyer's clerk.
$50,000	An actual appearance, in court, by the lawyer himself.
$100,000	Whatever it was you were hoping the first $500 would get you.
$250,000	A night of unspeakable pleasure with the lawyer's wife.
$1,000,000	The hand of the lawyer's daughter in marriage, his mother sold into slavery, his sons conscripted into a foreign army, his house, his soul and *this year's* calendar.

CHAPTER 6

Eighty Uses for Dead Lawyers

1. As curios to place on the mantelpiece.

**2. To test the theory that there are certain women
who could excite even a dead man.**

3. To ward off vampires.

**4. As drinking buddies who never start arguments,
never compete with one for a woman,
and can make one glass of beer last an eternity.**

5. As bait.

6. As yard-markers at football games.

7. As the only sort of lawyer you could trust with your wife, your watch or your wallet.

8. As companions for the disturbed.

9. For banks, as automatic cash machines in reverse.

10. As archery targets.

11. As unsanitary landfills.

12. As dummies for tailors and seamstresses.

13. As molds for Halloween masks.

**14. As statues for small impoverished towns
which can't afford to hire sculptors.**

15. For training proctologists.

16. For training dentists.

17. As abrasive elements for cleaning, construction, metalwork and chemical applications.

18. As Hollywood extras.

19. As ambassadors to small, unimportant countries where a real live ambassador would be wasted (in both senses of the word).

20. As pencil holders.

**21. As exhibits in Sunday schools,
for demonstrating the wages of deadly sins –
pride, covetousness, lust, anger, gluttony, envy, sloth.**

22. As large stringed instruments – where hollowness provides deep reverberation.

23. As 'dead wood' employees for major corporations who need more overpaid executives to do nothing.

24. As footrests.

25. As pincushions for home seamstresses.

26. For training watchdogs whom to attack.

27. As fencing material.

28. As doormen in cheap hotels.

29. For hearing confessions – especially of lawyers where a real live priest might die of shock.

30. As dartboards at the local bar.

31. As trash receptacles.

32. As food for the starving masses.

Lawyer loaf
2 lbs of lawyer, ground
2 cups of facts, shredded beyond recognition
1 dash of fantasy
1 handful of lies
1 small pinch of the truth (optional, for garnish)

Mix well. Bake in 350 degree oven for one hour.
Serve to in-laws and other guests whom you do not wish to return.

33. As punching bags at the local gymnasium.

34. As hallucinogenic drugs – take one lawyer-powder pill and lose the ability to distinguish between right and wrong, day and night, fact and fantasy.

35. As firewood.

36. To repopulate Death Valley, California.

37. As exercise equipment.

38. As practice dolls for schools of acupuncture.

39. As road signs to signify dead-end streets.

40. As bobsleds for winter sports.

41. As dead weight for navigational purposes.

42. As volleyball net holders.

43. As assistant acrobats.

44. In tractor-pulling contests.

**45. As rent-a-crowd, to help fill the house at an
unpopular play or concert.**

**46. As vacuum cleaners – they can still sniff out the dirt
when plugged in.**

47. As scarecrows.

48. As speed bumps.

49. For manning picket lines in labor disputes while the real employees are out doing what really works – slashing the bosses' tires and setting fire to the company's trucks.

50. As hatracks.

51. As demonstrators for boring ecological causes which attract no live demonstrators.

52. As condom dispensers in ladies' rooms.

53. For mushroom farming.

54. As ammunition for anti-aircraft guns.

55. For ring toss at carnival games.

56. As decoys when hunting wolves, who will mistake them for their own kind.

57. As building and insulation materials when wood and stone are in short supply.

58. As giant voodoo dolls.

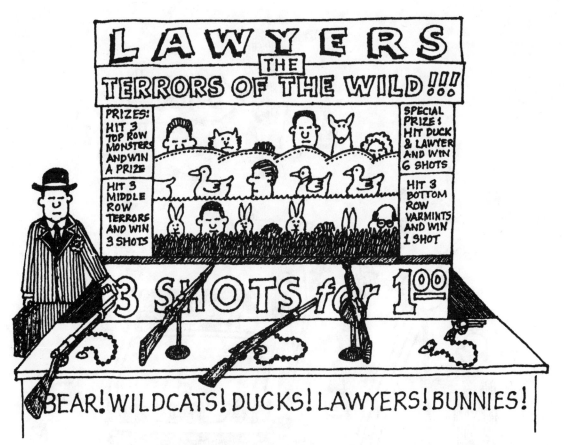

59. For the shooting gallery at carnival games.

60. As surgical sponges – good at sucking blood out of victims.

61. As road cones.

62. As doorknockers.

63. As landfill – but residences to be built at a safe distance to prevent contamination of occupants.

64. To provide shade for troops engaged in desert warfare.

65. As sandbags for terrorist attacks.

66. As sandbags for controlling flash floods.

67. To artificially inseminate animals.

68. For pressing flowers – cheaper and heavier than books and less likely to be missed.

69. As booby prizes at church raffles.

70. As a cheaper and more dependable way of killing rodents than traps.

71. As fly paper for country picnics – place at safe distance from picnic spot.

72. As flotation devices for scuba divers.

73. As auto-test crash dummies – cheaper than real dummies and less prone to breakage.

74. To be burned slowly like incense, as insect repellant in summertime.

75. As dance instructors for Englishmen.

76. As mannequins in shop windows, for overpriced but drab clothes with an abundance of loopholes.

77. As lawn ornaments for the rich and famous.

78. As metal detectors – lifeless hand will still grab for every coin buried within reach.

79. For offering less confusing advice than live lawyers.

80. As fertilizer when only pure, natural bullshit is acceptable.

CHAPTER 7

Legal Dictionary

ADVOCATE: A hired gun who will represent anyone, even a scumbag so low he couldn't reach a snake's belly, if there's enough money in it. Absent the large amounts of money paid to an advocate, such a person would normally be seen as an accessory or collaborator.

ATTORNEY: Also called 'attorney-at-law', this is simply another name for lawyer, counselor, solicitor, barrister, etc. and is just another of the many names behind which can hide that thief in the pinstripe suit who is helping himself to all of your hard-earned money.

BAR: Lawyers love the word bar and use it frequently in many different ways, possibly to further confuse their clients. (1) When a young attorney 'passes' the bar, he or she is formally admitted to that rogues' gallery known as the legal profession, and immediately gains the privilege of fleecing (see FLEECE) clients. (2) If various legalistic mumbo-jumbo does not transpire in accordance with various legal timetables, limitations and restrictions, an action may be 'barred' or prohibited. (3) An attorney who is caught doing the sorts of things that attorneys do best may wind up behind bars; and (4) as they age, most attorneys spend more and more of their time and more and more of their clients' money in bars.

BASTARD: A child born of unmarried parents or a lawyer. (A lawyer born of unmarried parents, a double bastard so to speak, is usually called a 'judge' (see JUDGE).

CLIENT: A lawyer's customer, basically, although lawyers feel that 'the client relationship' is one of such extreme trust and duty and honor that they prefer to never refer to their clients as customers. They do, however, refer to them as suckers, patsies and dupes.

CONSPIRATOR: A conspirator is one who, with others, plans to commit a crime and commences on the plan of action designed to effect the commission of that crime. This is not to be confused with 'partner' (see PARTNER), a senior member of a law firm who, with other partners, plans to extract a large sum of money (see RETAINER) from a rich client for questionable legal services and commences to do so in order to buy his daughter a Jaguar for her high school graduation present.

CRIMINAL: Among the lawyer's most favored clients are the criminals, or rather 'alleged criminals', who are always of course the victims of police misconduct or mistaken identity but who, interestingly enough, are always able to pay their lawyers handsomely in cash or video equipment still in the original carton.

DECISION: A decision is rendered by a court (see COURT – hey, wait a minute, I forgot to put COURT in the Legal Dictionary; well, I'll just slip it in right here – no one'll notice) after the judge goes into his chambers and flips a coin and then drinks for three hours to make it look like he was checking all those law books and thinking about the thing.

COURT: A big building with pillars and columns and gargoyles and statues and lots of polished wood and sneaky-looking guys with briefcases filled with money to give to judges so that the old coin-flip will come out the right way.

DEED: A deed is a piece of paper which is supposed to be filed someplace or other in order to show that a certain person is the owner of a certain piece of real property. Better make sure that your lawyer filed *your* deed instead of leaving it in his desk drawer for twenty years or drawing pictures on it to amuse the baby or maybe just lining the old birdcage with it or …

DEFENDANT:
(1) A perfectly innocent person who has been wrongly accused of a terrible criminal act of which he has no knowledge. (Above definition applies to those who have unlimited financial resources to hire an ADVOCATE.)

(2) The fellow who's going to be executed tomorrow. (This one's for everybody else.)

DOCUMENT: A document is really just a piece of paper, but by calling it a document the lawyer gets three thousand dollars for signing it.

EVIDENCE: Stuff that lawyers present to the court in order to prove that something did happen or something didn't happen. Generally, it goes like this: if your client did something he wasn't supposed to do, you go find, or make, some evidence showing that he didn't do it. But if he didn't do something he was supposed to do (like pay his taxes) you get some evidence to show that he *did* do what he was supposed to do, like an affidavit (see AFFIDAVIT – oh shit, I forgot to put that one in too – well, anyway, an affidavit is a formalized pack of lies signed and notarized by the affiant, who is the liar you paid to make the affidavit).

89

EXCLUSION: Exclusion is the rule by which evidence which has been wrongly obtained by the law enforcement authorities is excluded from the finder of fact (that's the judge or jury who'll be flipping the coin at the end of the case).

For example, suppose the police are looking for a man who's been kidnapping and boiling and eating the village's children. So let's say they get a tip from someone who saw the chap eating a small human leg with his morning croissant. The person calls the police and says: 'I saw him! Eating one of the children! He was driving a mauve delivery van!' So the police rush to the scene and they spot a lavender delivery van racing away. They stop it and discover the remains of ten or twenty wee ones inside. And then they arrest the driver of the van.

This is an outrage! A miscarriage of justice! This poor man must be released immediately! After all, anybody knows that mauve is a moderate shade of purple while lavender is a much paler shade of purple.

And so, the exclusionary rule works to protect all of us from the ravages and excesses of police misconduct.

FELON: A felon is a person who has been convicted of a felony. A felony is a major crime such as stealing a pen from the post office. Felonies are not to be confused with misdemeanors, which are minor crimes such as attacking people at random on the street, beating them senseless, and stealing their wallets and jewelry.

FLEECE: A lawyer's *raison d'etre*, his heart and soul, the light of his life, his alpha and omega, is, as you know, the retainer (SEE RETAINER). The act of taking the retainer off the client, that subtle and seductive art, that delicate surgery of words which results in the client's money magically becoming one with the lawyer's money, is known as fleecing, or 'the fleece'. To fleece a client, to obtain the retainer, brings the lawyer to a state of consciousness which is near orgasmic, but better!

GRAND JURY: The grand jury is nothing at all like a regular jury (see JURY). The grand jury is not only grander, but much simpler. While an ordinary jury actually has to sit through (or sleep through) a whole trial and hear evidence and weigh the pros and cons of whether or not to send a man to the electric chair and whether or not, more importantly, to order pizzas with or without pepperoni if the jury cannot reach a verdict (see VERDICT) before dinnertime, the grand jury only has to listen to the prosecutor (see PROSECUTOR) present the government's case and then do whatever the prosecutor wants or be stuck there for the next *year* eating pepperoni pizzas.

Thus, the grand jury acts to protect all of us from the capricious and arbitrary acts of elected officials who would use the powers of their offices to send those of us to prison who supported their opponents in the previous election.

GUARDIAN: A guardian acts *in loco parentis* (Latin for crazy parent) for a minor (person under the age of 18 or sometimes 21, depending on local laws) who is not his or her own child. The guardian's role is to protect the interests of that minor child by carefully investing most of the child's inheritance in highly-leveraged stock options and the remainder in building lots in Florida which the guardian has never actually seen. Also, the guardian develops a close emotional relationship with the minor by sending occasional postcards from the Mexican resort where he or she is staying while managing the minor's investments.

In order to prevent abuses of the very sacred duties which fall to the guardian, most guardians are appointed according to the wise and prudent decision-making of a judge (see JUDGE).

HIGH COURT: Depending on the jurisdiction, this may also be called the supreme court, superior court, court of appeals, etc. There may also be several levels of high court, and each succeeding level is able to overturn the decisions of those courts beneath it.

It is through appeals to the high court that lawyers are able to make a case go on almost forever, and insure that their clients will have every bit of due process that they are entitled to as long as they are able to keep paying for it.

Without high courts, cases would be resolved in a matter of five or six years instead of twenty or more. This would result in gross miscarriages of justice, and also hordes of hungry, fee-crazed lawyers roaming the streets and chanting menacingly in Latin.

INDICTMENT: An indictment is a criminal charge against an individual which is made by a grand jury after careful consideration of the prosecutor's personal grooming habits and after deliberating the scoring patterns in last night's ball game.

While an indictment is only an accusation, it immediately ruins one's reputation and costs everything one has to fight it, even if unsuccessful.

This, of course, is why there exist so many safeguards in our juridical system, particularly the grand jury (see GRAND JURY), to assure the rights of all innocent parties who can afford a lawyer.

JUDGE: A judge is a lawyer whose skills, education, experience, reputation and character are so exemplary that he or she has been elevated to a higher, god-like state – a judgeship. He will also have contributed heavily to the campaign fund of the politician who appointed him and dispensed favors 'from the bench' (the seat of a judge's power) to the politician's friends and relatives. But this is only a coincidence!

Judges wear black robes, but underneath those robes they wear many different sorts of things. Some lady judges wear only scanty little bits of lacy black lingerie and g-strings studded with rhinestones, or even nothing at all! And some men who are judges have nothing on underneath but scanty little bits of lacy black lingerie and g-strings studded with rhinestones, or nothing at all! Be careful! These are the judges who will have you sent to the electric chair fastest if you do anything to offend the public morals!

Most judges think they're big shots just because they can abuse anyone they want with total impunity and just because everyone grovels to them and treats them like gods. Well – wouldn't you? But just remember – not everyone can be a judge, so they should be respected. After all, it's not easy to drink for three hours during the lunchtime recess and still get those robes on frontwise!

JURISDICTION: Jurisdiction is a complex legal term which is often confused with 'venue' (see VENUE, but please see it in somebody else's dictionary because we don't have the space to put it in this one and even if we did we'd get it confused with 'jurisdiction' [see JURISDICTION] – hey, wait a minute, that's where we are now!) Jurisdiction is the area of legal interest over which a particular court may exercise authority.

Some courts are *criminal courts* and they put people on trial for crimes which they have been accused of committing, and then the courts send the innocent people off to subterranean dungeons and the guilty people on to lucrative media and entertainment contracts.

Other courts have no criminal jurisdiction but rather are *civil courts*. They hear such things as divorce cases and then decide to throw you out of your own house so that Annette, the adulterous bimbo you married, can live there in peace with her new boyfriend, Rocco (you remember Rocco, the fellow who used to be your chauffeur?).

Other courts are known as *petty courts*. These courts deal in chickenshit, basically, like parking tickets or summonses issued to you for walking your dog without a license. They don't even have real judges for these courts, but instead rely upon the skills and intelligence of a semi-literate baboon-like creature known as a magistrate, who might just as well be known as a magician because he pulls his verdicts out of thin air. So, this is what jurisdiction is all about, but sometimes it doesn't work the way it's supposed to.

There was once a man who was given a summons for driving his car too slowly down the main street, but because the policeman's writing was illegible, the man, named Mr Smith, went to the wrong courtroom. Another man, also named Mr Smith, had been accused of murder. Slow-driving Mr Smith identified himself and when asked how he pleaded said, 'Guilty as charged, your honor.' He was taken away in shackles and hanged the following Tuesday, despite his attempts to get someone to listen to his explanation about the summons. But there *is* a happy ending to this story. Murdering Mr Smith was also unable to find the correct courtroom and ended up in the traffic court instead. 'How do you plead?' asked the judge. 'Guilty as charged, your honor,' replied murdering Mr Smith. 'That'll be a twenty dollar fine, Mr Smith!' the judge admonished him. 'Here's forty!' replied murdering Mr Smith. 'For that price I'll take two!'

JURY: (see TRIAL, since that is where a jury does all of its damage and also since your typical jury member is just a simple-minded nobody whom nobody else cares about except when they're reading about all the stupid things that the jury did in the local newspaper. A jury shouldn't really have an entry of its own in a highbrow legal dictionary like this anyway!)

PARTNER: A partner is a lawyer who owns part of the law firm where he works (and the term 'works' is used very loosely in this definition). Other lawyers who work (and *really* work) at the law firm are called 'associates', but they don't own anything. Think of a beehive or an anthill and you'll start to get the picture. Remember how some of the ants are always carrying scuzzy-looking white things that are about ten times as big as they are and those ants never stop to rest until finally one day they just drop dead of exhaustion? And remember how some of the ants just stand around watching all the other ants and their only duties are to consume what the other ants have provided and maybe have sex with the female ants whenever they feel like it? Well, those ants who are just standing around watching are the *partners* in that anthill!

PROSECUTOR: Linguistics is a field which has always fascinated me (Elliott Egan, Esq, that is) because of the hidden meaning which can be found in so many words. Isn't it interesting how much 'prosecutor' and 'persecutor' sound like each other? Say either one ten times quickly and you'll likely wind up saying the other one. A prosecutor is a government attorney who attempts to gain criminal convictions against accused individuals, and then to send them to prison for a long while or to the gallows or electric chair for a very short while. Often a prosecutor will realize that the person accused of committing the crime could not possibly have done it, nevertheless the prosecutor just plows on ahead, ever vigilant against the innocent as well as the guilty! Prosecutors, like pitchers on professional baseball teams, are promoted and paid according to their wins in court. Nobody ever asks whether the right people got convicted – only how many!

RETAINER: A retainer is an exorbitant sum of money which is paid to a lawyer before he does any work in the hopes that he may do some work someday. This may seem illogical and unreasonable to the uneducated and unwashed masses who do not understand the intricacies and delicacies of the legal profession. The intricacies would include such things as the lawyer's expensive Swiss watch or the engine in his new Porsche. The delicacies would include caviar, vintage champagne, and truffles.

TRIAL: Modern version of medieval torture festival (wherein the accused was executed and dismembered first and tried later) which operates this way:

(1) Jury is picked from the local population of unemployed, infirm, insane, uneducated and otherwise useless individuals who are too stupid to know how to get out of serving on a jury, or, worse yet, actually *want* to serve on a jury.

(2) Twelve jury members are chosen because everybody knows that twelve idiots working together can make a better decision than one idiot working alone.

(3) Prosecutor, in his opening statements, calls defendant a scumbag and asks for the death penalty.

(4) Defense attorney, in his opening statements, calls prosecutor a scumbag and asks for the death penalty for *him*.

(5) The prosecution presents evidence and calls witnesses to prove that the defendant is guilty.

(6) The defense attorney calls defendant's friends and relatives as witnesses to testify that while the crime was being committed the defendant was in church with his mother, praying for the poor and elderly.

(7) The judge wakes up the jury and tells them to render a verdict.

(8) The jury asks the judge, 'What's a verdict?'

(9) The judge, having never been asked this before, looks dumbfounded and has his clerk look up 'verdict' in the Legal Dictionary section of this book, upon which the judge has relied for most of his legal training. Unfortunately, as this Legal Dictionary's last entry is 'trial', the clerk is unable to provide the judge with any assistance.

(10) The defendant, who has been on trial many times before, explains what a verdict is to the judge. The judge then explains it to the jury, but gets it wrong.

(11) The jury, hopelessly confused in addition to being stupid, finds the *prosecutor* guilty and sentences the *judge* to death.

(12) JUSTICE PREVAILS ONCE MORE!